MY ADVENTURES IN SCOTLAND

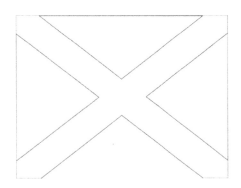

Travel Journal For Kids

Veropa Press
2019

The Ultimate Scotland Travel Journal For Kids: Writing Prompts and Activities For Scotland Adventures
ISBN: 9781073400058

This Travel Journal
Belongs To

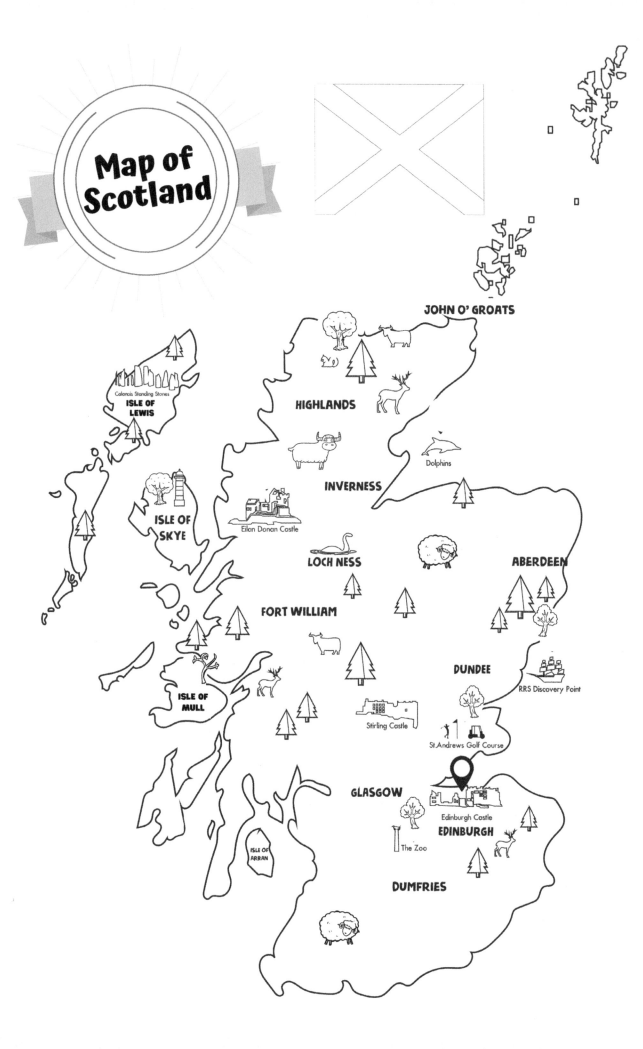

Map of Scotland

JOHN O' GROATS

HIGHLANDS

Calanais Standing Stones
ISLE OF LEWIS

Dolphins

ISLE OF SKYE

Eilan Donan Castle

INVERNESS

LOCH NESS

ABERDEEN

FORT WILLIAM

ISLE OF MULL

Stirling Castle

DUNDEE

RRS Discovery Point

St.Andrews Golf Course

GLASGOW

Edinburgh Castle

EDINBURGH

The Zoo

ISLE OF ARRAN

DUMFRIES

My Packing List

Make a list of the most important things you need to pack for your trip

Emergency Contact Information

Dad

email

Address

Mobile number

Mom

email

Address

Mobile number

Grandparents

email

Address

Mobile number

Other

email

Address

Mobile number

Itinerary and Hotel Information

#1 Location/Hotel

email

Address

Phone number

#2 Location/Hotel

email

Address

Phone number

#3 Location/Hotel

email

Address

Phone number

#4 Other

email

Address

Phone number

My Daily Journal

DATE

WHERE I AM TODAY

WEATHER TODAY

TODAY WE

SOMETHING I LEARNED TODAY

THE BEST PART OF THE DAY

THE WORST PART OF THE DAY

SOMETHING THAT MADE ME LAUGH

THE FOOD I ATE (WHAT I LIKED OR DISLIKED)

WHO WAS WITH US

RATE TODAY

DOODLE INSPIRED BY MY DAY

TODAY MY FAVOURITE MEMORY (DRAW OR STICK A PICTURE OR POSTCARD)

My Daily Journal

DATE

WHERE I AM TODAY

WEATHER TODAY

TODAY WE

SOMETHING I LEARNED TODAY

THE BEST PART OF THE DAY

THE WORST PART OF THE DAY

SOMETHING THAT MADE ME LAUGH

THE FOOD I ATE (WHAT I LIKED OR DISLIKED)

WHO WAS WITH US

RATE TODAY ⭐⭐⭐⭐⭐

DOODLE INSPIRED BY MY DAY

TODAY MY FAVOURITE MEMORY (DRAW OR STICK A PICTURE OR POSTCARD)

My Daily Journal

DATE _____

WHERE I AM TODAY _____

WEATHER TODAY

TODAY WE _____

_____

_____

_____

SOMETHING I LEARNED TODAY _____

_____

_____

THE BEST PART OF THE DAY _____

_____

THE WORST PART OF THE DAY _____

_____

SOMETHING THAT MADE ME LAUGH _____

_____

THE FOOD I ATE (WHAT I LIKED OR DISLIKED) _____

_____

_____

WHO WAS WITH US _____

_____

RATE TODAY ⭐ ⭐ ⭐ ⭐ ⭐

DOODLE INSPIRED BY MY DAY

TODAY MY FAVOURITE MEMORY (DRAW OR STICK A PICTURE OR POSTCARD)

My Daily Journal

DATE

WHERE I AM TODAY

WEATHER TODAY

TODAY WE

SOMETHING I LEARNED TODAY

THE BEST PART OF THE DAY

THE WORST PART OF THE DAY

SOMETHING THAT MADE ME LAUGH

THE FOOD I ATE (WHAT I LIKED OR DISLIKED)

WHO WAS WITH US

RATE TODAY

DOODLE INSPIRED BY MY DAY

TODAY MY FAVOURITE MEMORY (DRAW OR STICK A PICTURE OR POSTCARD)

My Daily Journal

DATE _____

WHERE I AM TODAY _____

WEATHER TODAY
_____

TODAY WE
_____
_____
_____
_____

SOMETHING I LEARNED TODAY
_____
_____

THE BEST PART OF THE DAY
_____

THE WORST PART OF THE DAY
_____

SOMETHING THAT MADE ME LAUGH
_____

THE FOOD I ATE (WHAT I LIKED OR DISLIKED)
_____
_____

WHO WAS WITH US
_____

RATE TODAY ⭐⭐⭐⭐⭐

DOODLE INSPIRED BY MY DAY

TODAY MY FAVOURITE MEMORY (DRAW OR STICK A PICTURE OR POSTCARD)

My Daily Journal

DATE

WHERE I AM TODAY

WEATHER TODAY

TODAY WE

SOMETHING I LEARNED TODAY

THE BEST PART OF THE DAY

THE WORST PART OF THE DAY

SOMETHING THAT MADE ME LAUGH

THE FOOD I ATE (WHAT I LIKED OR DISLIKED)

WHO WAS WITH US

RATE TODAY ⭐⭐⭐⭐⭐

DOODLE INSPIRED BY MY DAY

TODAY MY FAVOURITE MEMORY (DRAW OR STICK A PICTURE OR POSTCARD)

My Daily Journal

DATE

WHERE I AM TODAY

WEATHER TODAY

TODAY WE

SOMETHING I LEARNED TODAY

THE BEST PART OF THE DAY

THE WORST PART OF THE DAY

SOMETHING THAT MADE ME LAUGH

THE FOOD I ATE (WHAT I LIKED OR DISLIKED)

WHO WAS WITH US

RATE TODAY

DOODLE INSPIRED BY MY DAY

TODAY MY FAVOURITE MEMORY (DRAW OR STICK A PICTURE OR POSTCARD)

My Daily Journal

DATE _____

WHERE I AM TODAY _____

WEATHER TODAY
_____

TODAY WE _____

_____

_____

_____

SOMETHING I LEARNED TODAY _____

_____

_____

THE BEST PART OF THE DAY _____

_____

THE WORST PART OF THE DAY _____

_____

SOMETHING THAT MADE ME LAUGH _____

_____

THE FOOD I ATE (WHAT I LIKED OR DISLIKED) _____

_____

_____

_____

WHO WAS WITH US _____

_____

RATE TODAY ⭐⭐⭐⭐⭐

DOODLE INSPIRED BY MY DAY

TODAY MY FAVOURITE MEMORY (DRAW OR STICK A PICTURE OR POSTCARD)

My Daily Journal

DATE

WHERE I AM TODAY

WEATHER TODAY

TODAY WE

SOMETHING I LEARNED TODAY

THE BEST PART OF THE DAY

THE WORST PART OF THE DAY

SOMETHING THAT MADE ME LAUGH

THE FOOD I ATE (WHAT I LIKED OR DISLIKED)

WHO WAS WITH US

RATE TODAY

DOODLE INSPIRED BY MY DAY

TODAY MY FAVOURITE MEMORY (DRAW OR STICK A PICTURE OR POSTCARD)

My Daily Journal

DATE _____

WHERE I AM TODAY _____

WEATHER TODAY

TODAY WE _____

_____

_____

_____

_____

SOMETHING I LEARNED TODAY _____

_____

_____

THE BEST PART OF THE DAY _____

_____

THE WORST PART OF THE DAY _____

_____

SOMETHING THAT MADE ME LAUGH _____

_____

THE FOOD I ATE (WHAT I LIKED OR DISLIKED) _____

_____

_____

_____

WHO WAS WITH US _____

RATE TODAY ⭐⭐⭐⭐⭐

DOODLE INSPIRED BY MY DAY

TODAY MY FAVOURITE MEMORY (DRAW OR STICK A PICTURE OR POSTCARD)

My Daily Journal

DATE

WHERE I AM TODAY

WEATHER TODAY

TODAY WE

SOMETHING I LEARNED TODAY

THE BEST PART OF THE DAY

THE WORST PART OF THE DAY

SOMETHING THAT MADE ME LAUGH

THE FOOD I ATE (WHAT I LIKED OR DISLIKED)

WHO WAS WITH US

RATE TODAY ★★★★★

DOODLE INSPIRED BY MY DAY

TODAY MY FAVOURITE MEMORY (DRAW OR STICK A PICTURE OR POSTCARD)

My Daily Journal

DATE

WHERE I AM TODAY

WEATHER TODAY

TODAY WE

SOMETHING I LEARNED TODAY

THE BEST PART OF THE DAY

THE WORST PART OF THE DAY

SOMETHING THAT MADE ME LAUGH

THE FOOD I ATE (WHAT I LIKED OR DISLIKED)

WHO WAS WITH US

RATE TODAY ⭐⭐⭐⭐⭐

DOODLE INSPIRED BY MY DAY

TODAY MY FAVOURITE MEMORY (DRAW OR STICK A PICTURE OR POSTCARD)

My Daily Journal

DATE _____

WHERE I AM TODAY _____

WEATHER TODAY

TODAY WE _____

_____

_____

_____

SOMETHING I LEARNED TODAY _____

_____

_____

THE BEST PART OF THE DAY _____

_____

THE WORST PART OF THE DAY _____

_____

SOMETHING THAT MADE ME LAUGH _____

_____

THE FOOD I ATE (WHAT I LIKED OR DISLIKED) _____

_____

_____

WHO WAS WITH US _____

RATE TODAY ⭐⭐⭐⭐⭐

DOODLE INSPIRED BY MY DAY

TODAY MY FAVOURITE MEMORY (DRAW OR STICK A PICTURE OR POSTCARD)

My Daily Journal

DATE _____

WHERE I AM TODAY _____

WEATHER TODAY

TODAY WE _____

_____

_____

_____

_____

SOMETHING I LEARNED TODAY _____

_____

_____

THE BEST PART OF THE DAY _____

_____

THE WORST PART OF THE DAY _____

_____

SOMETHING THAT MADE ME LAUGH _____

_____

THE FOOD I ATE (WHAT I LIKED OR DISLIKED) _____

_____

_____

WHO WAS WITH US _____

_____

RATE TODAY ⭐⭐⭐⭐⭐

DOODLE INSPIRED BY MY DAY

TODAY MY FAVOURITE MEMORY (DRAW OR STICK A PICTURE OR POSTCARD)

My Daily Journal

DATE _____

WHERE I AM TODAY _____

WEATHER TODAY

_____

TODAY WE

_____
_____
_____
_____

SOMETHING I LEARNED TODAY

_____
_____
_____

THE BEST PART OF THE DAY

_____
_____

THE WORST PART OF THE DAY

_____
_____

SOMETHING THAT MADE ME LAUGH

_____
_____

THE FOOD I ATE (WHAT I LIKED OR DISLIKED)

_____
_____
_____

WHO WAS WITH US

_____
_____

RATE TODAY ⭐⭐⭐⭐⭐

DOODLE INSPIRED BY MY DAY

TODAY MY FAVOURITE MEMORY (DRAW OR STICK A PICTURE OR POSTCARD)

My Daily Journal

DATE

WHERE I AM TODAY

WEATHER TODAY

TODAY WE

SOMETHING I LEARNED TODAY

THE BEST PART OF THE DAY

THE WORST PART OF THE DAY

SOMETHING THAT MADE ME LAUGH

THE FOOD I ATE (WHAT I LIKED OR DISLIKED)

WHO WAS WITH US

RATE TODAY

★★★★★

DOODLE INSPIRED BY MY DAY

TODAY MY FAVOURITE MEMORY (DRAW OR STICK A PICTURE OR POSTCARD)

My Daily Journal

DATE

WHERE I AM TODAY

WEATHER TODAY

TODAY WE

SOMETHING I LEARNED TODAY

THE BEST PART OF THE DAY

THE WORST PART OF THE DAY

SOMETHING THAT MADE ME LAUGH

THE FOOD I ATE (WHAT I LIKED OR DISLIKED)

WHO WAS WITH US

RATE TODAY ★★★★★

DOODLE INSPIRED BY MY DAY

TODAY MY FAVOURITE MEMORY (DRAW OR STICK A PICTURE OR POSTCARD)

My Daily Journal

DATE

WHERE I AM TODAY

WEATHER TODAY

TODAY WE

SOMETHING I LEARNED TODAY

THE BEST PART OF THE DAY

THE WORST PART OF THE DAY

SOMETHING THAT MADE ME LAUGH

THE FOOD I ATE (WHAT I LIKED OR DISLIKED)

WHO WAS WITH US

RATE TODAY

DOODLE INSPIRED BY MY DAY

TODAY MY FAVOURITE MEMORY (DRAW OR STICK A PICTURE OR POSTCARD)

My Daily Journal

DATE

WHERE I AM TODAY

WEATHER TODAY

TODAY WE

SOMETHING I LEARNED TODAY

THE BEST PART OF THE DAY

THE WORST PART OF THE DAY

SOMETHING THAT MADE ME LAUGH

THE FOOD I ATE (WHAT I LIKED OR DISLIKED)

WHO WAS WITH US

RATE TODAY

DOODLE INSPIRED BY MY DAY

TODAY MY FAVOURITE MEMORY (DRAW OR STICK A PICTURE OR POSTCARD)

My Daily Journal

DATE _____

WHERE I AM TODAY _____

WEATHER TODAY _____

TODAY WE _____

_____

_____

_____

_____

SOMETHING I LEARNED TODAY _____

_____

_____

THE BEST PART OF THE DAY _____

_____

THE WORST PART OF THE DAY _____

_____

SOMETHING THAT MADE ME LAUGH _____

_____

THE FOOD I ATE (WHAT I LIKED OR DISLIKED) _____

_____

_____

WHO WAS WITH US _____

_____

RATE TODAY ⭐⭐⭐⭐⭐

DOODLE INSPIRED BY MY DAY

TODAY MY FAVOURITE MEMORY (DRAW OR STICK A PICTURE OR POSTCARD)

My Daily Journal

DATE _____

WHERE I AM TODAY _____

WEATHER TODAY

TODAY WE _____

_____

_____

_____

_____

SOMETHING I LEARNED TODAY _____

_____

_____

THE BEST PART OF THE DAY _____

_____

THE WORST PART OF THE DAY _____

_____

SOMETHING THAT MADE ME LAUGH _____

_____

THE FOOD I ATE (WHAT I LIKED OR DISLIKED) _____

_____

_____

WHO WAS WITH US _____

_____

RATE TODAY ⭐⭐⭐⭐⭐

DOODLE INSPIRED BY MY DAY

TODAY MY FAVOURITE MEMORY (DRAW OR STICK A PICTURE OR POSTCARD)

My Vacation Favourites

Place

Food

Activity

Sight

My Gifts List

Make a list of unique souvenirs for your friends and family

Edinburgh
Christmas Market
It is held at East Princes
Street Gardens

It offers 6 week of festive entertainment,
shopping experience and
gastronomic surprises

The Royal Mile is Edinburgh's most famous street. It connects Edinburgh Castle with Holyrood Palace.

The bagpipe is the national instrument of Scotland

Edinburgh Zoo is home to over 1,000 rare and endangered animals, including the UK's only giant pandas, koalas, sun bears, Indian Rhinos, chimpanzees, sloths, penguins, etc.

EDINBURGH ZOO

ZOO

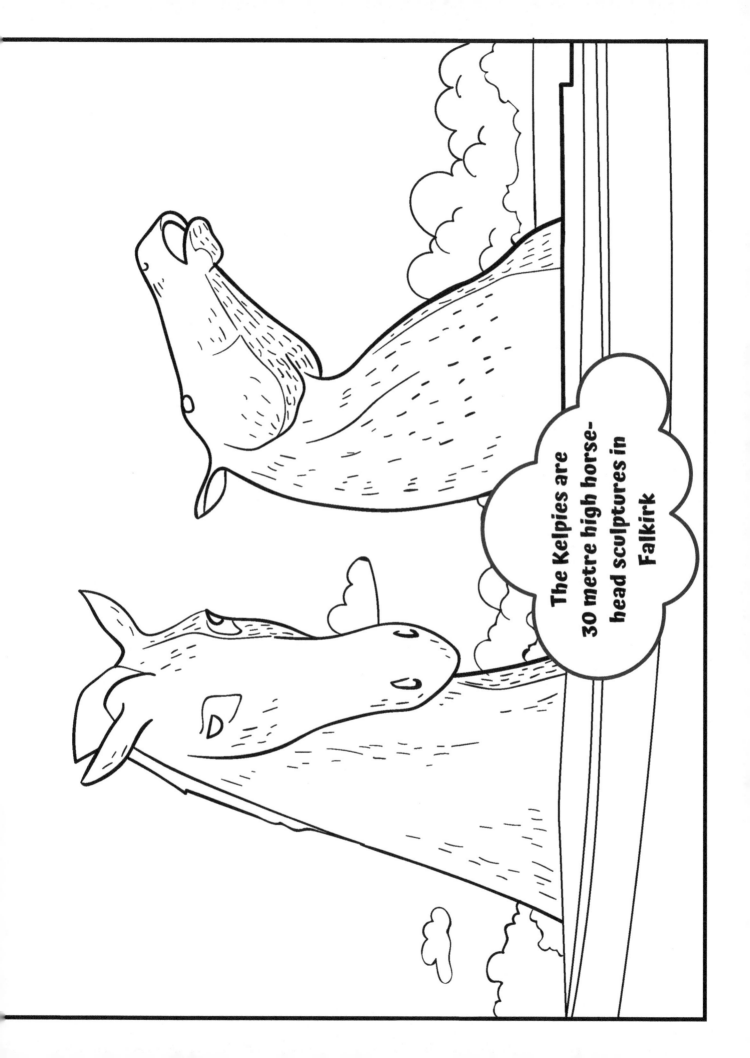

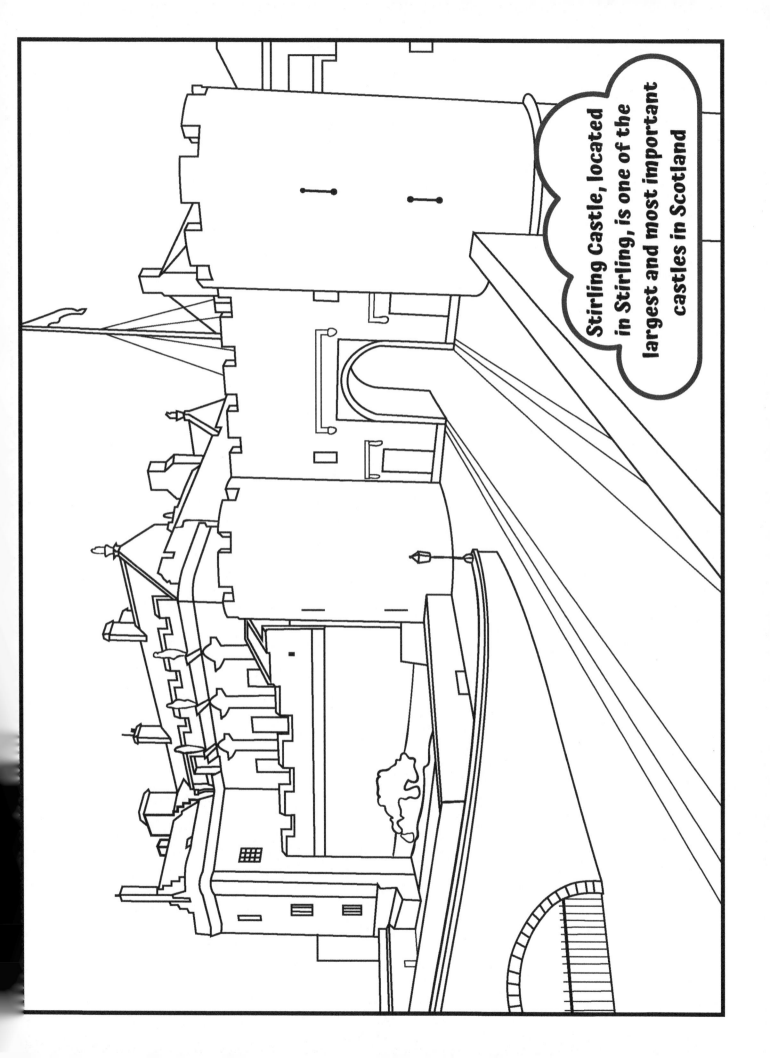

Dunnottar Castle is a ruined medieval fortress located on a rocky headland on the northeastern coast of Scotland, about 2 miles south of Stonehaven. The ruins of the castle are spread over 1.4 hectares (3.5 acres), surrounded by steep cliffs that drop to the North Sea, 160 feet (49 m) below.

Scotland Crossword

Across

2. specific textile pattern that typically denotes a particular Scottish clan

4. musical instrument that is typical for Scotland

8. nickname for Scottish Terrier

9. Scottish cow breed

10. the name of the famous monster that lives in Loch Ness

Down

1. one of the most traditional and recognisable Scottish dish

3. Scotland's biggest city

5. the capital city of Scotland

6. a floral emblem of Scotland

7. the national Scottish animal

VOCABULARY - NEW WORDS I HAVE LEARNED

VOCABULARY - NEW WORDS I HAVE LEARNED

GLUE OR TAPE BOARDING PASSES

GLUE OR TAPE MAPS, PICTURES FROM LEAFLETS, GUIDES OR BROCHURES

GLUE OR TAPE RESTAURANT CARDS, POSTCARDS, ETC

GLUE OR TAPE TICKETS FROM ENTRY TO MUSEUMS, GALLERIES, ETC.

Made in United States
North Haven, CT
02 March 2023

33383289R00057